THE
FIRST
WORLD WAR
IN
POSTERS

Daddy, what did *YOU* do in the Great War?

PUBLISHED BY THE PARLIAMENTARY RECRUITING COMMITTEE, LONDON. POSTER NO 79.   DESIGNED AND PRINTED BY JOHNSON, RIDDLE & CO., LTD., LONDON, S.E.

THE FIRST WORLD WAR IN POSTERS

FROM THE
IMPERIAL WAR MUSEUM, LONDON

SELECTED AND EDITED BY
JOSEPH DARRACOTT

ASSISTANT DIRECTOR AND KEEPER OF THE DEPARTMENT OF ART,
IMPERIAL WAR MUSEUM

DOVER PUBLICATIONS, INC., NEW YORK

ACKNOWLEDGMENTS

I am grateful to many colleagues at the Imperial War Museum for help with this publication; I particularly wish to mention Mr. F. J. Dicker, Dr. C. Dowling, Mr. B. E. L. Kitts, Mr. D. P. Mayne, Mr. M. D. Moody, Mr. J. O. S. Simmonds and Mr. B. D. Slade. It has been good to be able to choose both famous and little-known posters and to have them expertly photographed. I should also like to thank the staff of Dover Publications and Mrs. Roberta W. Wong in New York. Finally, my thanks go to Miss Belinda Loftus, my former colleague and co-author, whose sound knowledge of posters much enriched our joint work and hence this book.

Published in Canada by General Publishing Company, Ltd., 30 Lesmill Road, Don Mills, Toronto, Ontario.
Published in the United Kingdom by Constable and Company, Ltd., 3 The Lanchesters, 162–164 Fulham Palace Road, London W6 9ER.

The First World War in Posters is a new work, first published by Dover Publications, Inc., in 1974.

International Standard Book Number: 0-486-22979-3
Library of Congress Catalog Card Number: 73-94348

Manufactured in the United States of America
Dover Publications, Inc.
31 East 2nd Street
Mineola, N.Y. 11501

INTRODUCTION

The First World War made greater demands on the physical and human resources of the nations involved than had ever been dreamt necessary before. It was a war of industrial competition, in which the manufacture of arms and munitions became critically important; it was a war in which recent inventions like the Zeppelin, the airplane or the machine gun were used with deadly effect and a new invention, the tank, made its appearance. It was also a war in which the wills of whole nations had to be engaged: information about the war was needed, and had to be supplied by traditional means, such as newspapers, proclamations and notices; newer media were also required, like film, and pictorial posters, which were able to persuade as well as inform.

The modern poster had become a valuable means of commercial promotion by the end of the nineteenth century. In the 1890s posters were drawn by outstanding artists like Toulouse-Lautrec, Chéret, Mucha and the Beggarstaffs. The early years of the twentieth century saw a new generation of able men, among them Hohlwein. Posters were reproduced and became popular as art prints and collected; the general public became accustomed to seeing posters in the streets, and on the hoardings of building sites. By the time the First World War broke out, posters were as well established as press advertising; it would have been folly for governments to have neglected such a successful medium.

Governments exploited posters; they were used to call for recruits (in America and Australia, and in Britain until conscription was instituted in 1916), to request war loans, to make national policies acceptable, to spur industrial effort, to channel emotions such as courage or hate, to urge conservation of resources and inform the public of food and fuel substitutes. Charitable organizations requested financial support for disabled fighting men, prisoners of war and civilian casualties. The posters reproduced in the present volume include outstanding examples of all these types, as well as some more specialized posters; there is a poster designed as an inspiring gift to the men in the trenches, another which advertises one of the many exhibitions of war drawings, and even a commercial poster for candy that identifies its proved merit with that of the army.

Although posters are here seen in isolation, it should be recalled that they were often employed as part of a bigger campaign, together with personal appearances by celebrities, pageants, house-to-house calls, the launching of popular songs, press advertising, flag days, badges, as well as posters in huge format occupying a whole hoarding.

National campaigns needed to be much more extensive than those for commercial products. Between 1914 and 1918 millions of posters were printed and displayed in every country. The campaigns in the United States were the biggest. For the First Liberty Loan, two million posters were printed; for the Second Liberty Loan, there were five million posters; for the Third Liberty Loan, nine million posters were produced. European campaigns were not on quite the same massive scale, although photographs of cities during the war show how dominating were the hoardings on which Lord Kitchener appeared, or in Italy a soldier in the same pose appealing for money.

There were various means of distributing posters. In Britain an unusual method was adopted. The political parties combined to form a Parliamentary Recruiting Committee (whose greatest success was the Kitchener poster), and this committee used local party organizations as a means of distribution.

The style of a First World War poster may mainly depend on one of three factors: the designer may continue to develop his own personal style; national imagery, or a particular national appeal may be used; or an international style like Art Nouveau may be employed.

In America, certain magazine and book illustrators were so popular that they played a dominant role in the production of war posters even though they had not previously been identified with poster art. James Montgomery Flagg's Uncle Sam, one of the most widely reproduced images in history (five million copies are said to have been printed), was a self-portrait. Cheerful glamor was contributed by Howard Chandler Christy, whose Christy Girl enticed men to join the Navy. The black-and-white illustrator Joseph Pennell, friend and biographer of Whistler, turned his lithographic ability to equally patriotic use. Some of the best-known American illustrators were organized by Charles Dana Gibson in the Division of Pictorial Publicity, which produced posters on demand for government departments. This work was done free, and one of the illustrators commented: "They are big men who would ordinarily receive $1000 to $10,000 for a sketch, so you can see what the nation is saving."

Such patriotic generosity was widespread, and points to the very general involvement of the whole community in the war.

Although illustrators were not so predominant in other countries as America, they were widely used. Popular cartoonists' work was sometimes printed as it stood, but the results were not always as satisfactory as Partridge's "Soldiers All" from *Punch*, or the meticulous realism of "Good-Bye, Old Man" by Fortunino Matania. The change of scale from magazine illustration to poster could pose a problem for an illustrator; it is instructive to see that a propagandist so skilled as Raemaekers abandoned the sketchy treatment of his cartoons for a bolder composition in the poster "In Belgium—Help." Some French illustrators succeeded with strongly drawn images like "On Les Aura!" and, as in America, characters from magazines were pressed into war service; the Christy Girl is paralleled by Poulbot's irreverent small boys from his prewar cartoons, to whose characterization he added a twinge of pathos. A few illustrators went deeper than realism and beyond patriotism. Steinlen is one of those few: his sombre war posters are mainly appeals for the casualties of war, such as the justly famous "Sur la Terre Ennemie."

Illustration is not the only possible approach to poster design, and it did not stand preeminent in Austria and Germany. A single dominant image was the hallmark of a commercial poster there before the war, and so it remained in war posters. In McKnight Kauffer's book *The Art of the Poster*, many sources of single images for poster designers are given, such as silhouettes, memorial brasses and Japanese woodcuts; Toulouse-Lautrec is described as "The Prophet of the Modern Poster" because of his ability to simplify, and praise is given to the Beggarstaffs (William Nicholson and James Pryde), to whose work Hohlwein owed a debt. An effective example of a single image was the head of Hindenburg by Oppenheim, which had a popularity comparable with that of Lord Kitchener or Uncle Sam. However, dominant images could also be more abstract, as in the U in Erdt's U-boat poster, or the figure 8 in Klinger's Eighth War Loan poster.

Despite these personal and national preferences, much poster art was international, since the designers had so many common problems. Long before the war, Berlin, London, Munich, Paris and Vienna had all become important centers for poster designers, and magazines like *The Poster* (United States), *The Studio* (Great Britain) and *Das Plakat* (Germany) kept up to date with developments abroad. Poster designers moved about: Bernhard went to Berlin from Vienna to practice; Pennell made his home in London, where Hohlwein studied (like Jules Chéret before him) and Oppenheim practiced; and Biró won a poster competition organized by *The Studio* in 1910. Cappiello was attracted from Italy, and Steinlen from Switzerland, to make their careers in Paris; Parisian students included Biró, Flagg, Karpellus, Leyendecker and Spencer Pryse. Poster plagiarism was rife—*Das Plakat* issued a special edition in 1914 of plagiarized commercial images, showing such examples as a German poster adapted for the cover of *The Poster*, and a German plagiarism of an American advertisement. Poster competitions and exhibitions were held in every country before the war. Quite a number of war poster exhibitions were held during the war; some examples are *British Recruiting Posters* (Berlin, 1915), *Italian Artists and the Front* (including poster designs; London, 1916), *Russian War Posters* (Plaza Hotel, New York, 1917) and *Posters of All the Belligerent Nations* (Neuilly, 1917).

Posters echoed the international character of art at that time. The brilliant international style of Art Nouveau lingers on in some war posters, such as that by Zasche; it is reflected in the decorative detail of Lefler's work and in Coles Phillips' design, but had been abandoned by Erler, one of the co-founders of the magazine *Die Jugend*, which gave its name to *Jugendstil* (the German name for the style). Post-Impressionism is reflected in the poster by Suján. More experimental styles were less commonly used for war posters, although they could be decidedly effective, as can be seen in the exhibition posters for Paul Nash, Wolmark or Nevinson, whose adaptation of Futurist means is especially successful. Again, some posters are less national than in the main tradition of academic European painting, like the work of Fouqueray or of another mural painter, Brangwyn.

As for the content and imagery of First World War posters, Lord Kitchener and Uncle Sam are certainly the best-known figures from the gallery, partly because they have been so widely copied and imitated. There were many versions of the Kitchener poster, and the pose was taken up in posters round the world. Even during the Second World War the pose was reused, Lord Kitchener's pointing finger being replaced by Churchill's. Kitchener himself slept like some Rip Van Winkle until he woke bewildered and misunderstood in the nineteen sixties. His face then became common currency in London's souvenir markets advertising such things as a clothes shop called "I Was Lord Kitchener's Valet."

The problem of those designers who wished to use a single image was sometimes solved by using a flag. In Britain the national flag was used to arouse patriotism, while in German hands a torn British flag symbolized the destruction of British power. The American flag was a potent symbol of unity, although it is interesting to see that appeals to old loyalties were also made, as in the poster showing Czechoslovakian flags designed by Vojtech Pressig.

Other national symbols were valuable to designers,

although they may not always have been so easy to use in a poster composition. There is something of a tour de force in the way in which Lefler or Gipkens used the Imperial eagle, or in which Capon and Dorival made it the target for anti-German feeling. Personifications of the nations, like Uncle Sam, John Bull and Britannia, lend themselves more to cartoon treatment than to emotive appeals, although there are exceptional cases like Georges Scott's heroic figure of Marianne. An irony of religious symbolism is that it could be and was used by both sides—there are posters of St. George and the Dragon from Britain, Russia and Austria.

Some posters also echo or exploit references to art-historical sources. Foringer's "Greatest Mother in the World" has religious overtones: the upturned head was a feature of pictures of the Virgin Mary from the time of Raphael; the pyramidical composition recalls groups of the Virgin and Child; the fact that the figure of the soldier is on a stretcher makes an allusion to paintings of Mary with the body of the dead Christ. The feeling of familiarity with these images is clearly part of the poster's appeal, although the nature of the appeal may not be fully understood. Faivre's "On Les Aura!" also makes an allusion to a well-known image, the figure of Marianne on the Arc de Triomphe. Occasionally, other sorts of references are made to less sophisticated arts, such as the popular nineteenth-century prints which make a base for Hansi's charming style. German artists also used popular prints as sources of imagery, but in some cases, say the poster by Boehle, the reference is more specifically national, a way of asserting the importance of the German graphic tradition from the days of Dürer.

At first sight, there would seem to be no possible sources for some of the most unpleasant war posters, designed to incite anger and hatred. This sort of propaganda was not used in Germany and Austria; it was mainly used in Britain and America. There are some barbarous American images of German atrocities, including children with their hands cut off, illustrating stories of the sort which were shown after the war to have been quite unfounded in fact. There were also some vicious anti-German images produced in France, although the Imperial War Museum has more prints than posters in this category.

Almost no posters are without text, so that typography is a constant factor in poster design. The most distinguished typography to be found in war posters is German or Austrian, since many of the designers, such as Bernhard or Klinger, also designed typefaces. In addition, some effective designs were made solely from type, such as that by Ranzenhofer. French typography, while rarely exceptional, has the professional standard that one would expect from the highly competent lithographic ateliers in Paris. Some British typography is of an acceptable standard, such as the

posters executed for the London Underground, but from a typographical point of view, the Parliamentary Recruiting Committee posters were generally poor, since decisions about type seem to have been often left to the printers. American typography was of a sound standard, although a committee decision could damage a design, as was the case in Pennell's image of New York in flames, for which he had chosen an apter and simpler slogan than was actually used.

To look at a group of First World War posters together, as in this volume, is to sense the immediate response which they inspired. Their unabashed sentiment would not be possible today; personal appeals— "I want *you*," "What did *you* do?"—were widespread. These posters, too, give a many-sided image of war and its effects—the weariness of the soldier, the dejection of the prisoner, the destruction of cities and disruption of normal life.

These posters are also valuable as historical documents. Our idea of the First World War is darkly colored by our knowledge of the tragedy of the battle-fields. Posters can give some idea of the flavor of the period as it was experienced by civilians. If we are astounded at the psychological approach of recruiting posters in 1914, that is mainly due to a historical misunderstanding which posters can help to correct. In these posters there are old feelings we could not know in any other way.

It is now impossible to estimate the effectiveness of war posters as against such other media as press advertising and films (toward the end of the war, the cinema played a more important part in conveying information and influencing opinion). The popular success of a poster can only be measured by its wide use and frequency of reprinting; this has to be distinguished from an artistic success, such as Spear's "Enlist," which is striking and well known today, but originally had only a small circulation. Almost all that we can say is that posters helped to raise substantial numbers of recruits and extremely large sums of money.

The propaganda of the Nazi party learned important lessons from the posters of the First World War. Hitler believed that the artistic quality of the German and Austrian posters was not appreciated by the general public, and that the simpler messages of British and American posters were more effective. He wrote in *Mein Kampf:* "All effective propaganda must be confined to a few bare essentials and those must be expressed as far as possible in stereotyped formulas," and commented that propaganda "must fix its intellectual level so as not to be above the heads of the least intellectual of those to whom it is directed." A similar moral was drawn by commercial organizations, which began increasingly to take into account the results of market surveys, and to rely less on artistic reputation alone.

Joseph Darracott   ix

Looking at the postwar history of advertising, we now realize that the war was a watershed for this important industry. First, it provided a memorable example of the effective organization of advertising. Secondly, a psychological approach was to become the rule, not the exception, of postwar publicity. The methods evolved in the First World War to inform and persuade all the people are still in use.

BOOKS

There is no thorough modern study of First World War posters.

The Imperial War Museum has a file of bibliographical references, but few items are specifically about war posters. The following selection includes general surveys and some of the books consulted for the present publication.

Arnold, Friedrich, *Deutsche Plakate als Dokumente der Zeit 1900–1960*, 1963.

Creel, George, *How We Advertised America*, New York, 1920.

Darracott, Joseph, and Loftus, Belinda, *First World War Posters*, London, 1972.

Fehl, Philipp, and Fenix, Patricia, *World War I Propaganda Posters*, Chapel Hill, 1969.

Hardie, Martin, and Sabin, Arthur K., *War Posters Issued by Belligerent Nations 1914–1919*, London, 1920.

Harper, Paula, *War Revolution and Peace*, Palo Alto, 1971.

Kauffer, E. McKnight, *The Art of the Poster*, London, 1924.

Massiczek, Albert, and Sagl, Hermann, *Zeit an der Wand*, Vienna, 1967.

Pennell, Joseph, *The Liberty Loan Poster*, New York, 1919.

Rickards, Maurice, *Posters of the First World War*, London, 1969.

Rubetti, G., *Un'Arma per la vittoria*, Milan, 1917.

Rubetti, G., *La Pubblicità nei prestiti italiani di guerra*, Milan, 1919.

The main periodicals to be consulted are: for France, *L'Affiche et les arts de la publicité* (a war posters number, 1928); for Germany, *Das Plakat*; for Great Britain, *The Placard* (1914–1916; resumed publication after the war); for the United States of America, *The Poster*.

LIST OF ILLUSTRATIONS

The entries in this list give the following information in the following order:
  Artist's name; nationality; title of poster (short version of title, in English); dimensions of poster in inches and in centimeters, height before width.

Frontispiece: SAVILE LUMLEY (British): "Daddy, What Did *You* Do in the Great War?"; 30 × 20 in., 76.3 × 50.8 cm.

COLOR

BLACK AND WHITE

THE
FIRST
WORLD WAR
IN
POSTERS

PESTI NAPLÓ

RICHTER & Co
NAPOLI

"FINALMENTE!"

VI.º
PRESTITO
NAZIONALE

2   Mario Borgoni: "At Last!"

PUT STRENGTH IN
THE FINAL BLOW
BUY WAR BONDS.

4   T. Butschkin: "Freedom Loan"

L'ARMEE SUISSE

Helft uns siegen!

zeichnet
die
Kriegsanleihe

Entwurf: Prof. Fritz Erler, München. Druck: Hollerbaum & Schmidt, Berlin N.

MUST
CHILDREN DIE
AND MOTHERS
PLEAD IN VAIN
?

Buy More
LIBERTY BONDS

On les aura !

2ᴱ EMPRUNT
DE
LA DÉFENSE NATIONALE

Souscrivez

DEVAMBEZ Imp PARIS

BOOKS
WANTED
FOR OUR MEN
"IN CAMP AND
OVER THERE"
TAKE YOUR GIFTS TO
THE PUBLIC LIBRARY

LE CARDINAL MERCIER PROTEGE LA BELGIQUE

LAPINA. IMP. PARIS.

14   DOMINIQUE CHARLES FOUQUERAY: "Cardinal Mercier Protects Belgium"

...Ce ciel est notre azur
Ce champ est notre terre!
Cette Lorraine
et cette Alsace,
c'est à Nous!
Victor Hugo.

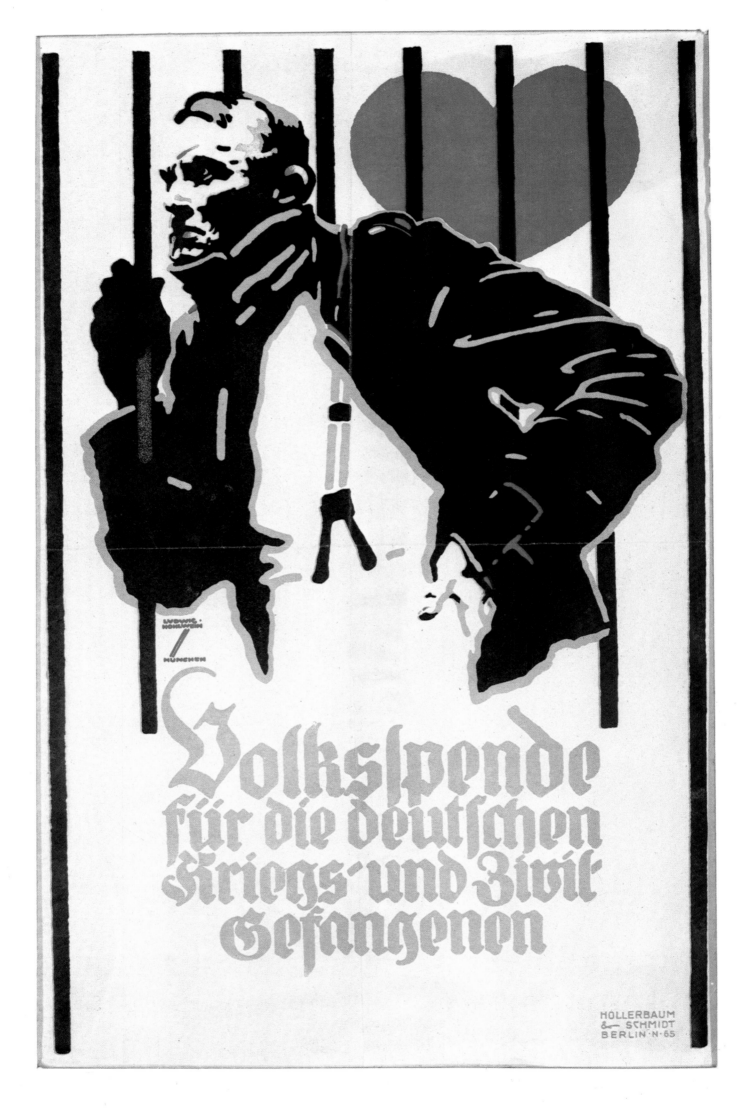

Volksspende
für die deutschen
Kriegs-und Zivil-
Gefangenen

20 LUDWIG HOHLWEIN: "People's Charity for Prisoners of War"

JOURNÉE DE L'ARMÉE D'AFRIQUE
ET DES TROUPES COLONIALES

DEVAMBEZ, PARIS

22 Lucien-Hector Jonas: "African Army Day"

ADOLF KARPELLUS: "Subscribe to the Seventh War Loan"   23

ZEICH·NET

4.KRIEGSANLEIHE

K·K HOF· J.WEINER WIEN

26   HEINRICH LEFLER: "Subscribe to the Fourth War Loan"

OTTO LEHMANN: "Support Our Men in Uniform"   27

1914 — 1917

Zeichnet die Sechste Kriegsanleihe

28 MAXIMILIAN LENZ: "Subscribe to the Sixth War Loan"

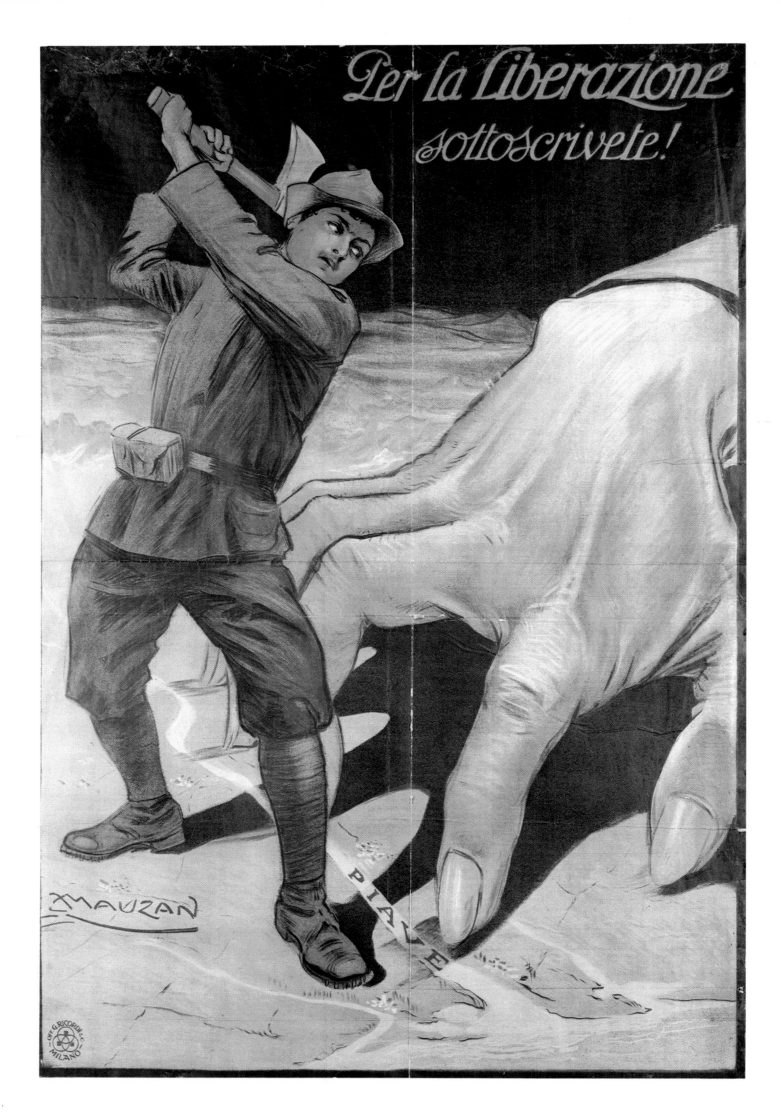

Luciano Achille Mauzan: "For Liberation, Subscribe!"

ON NE PASSE PAS!
1914   1918

Par deux fois j'ai tenu et vaincu sur la Marne,
Civil, mon frère,
La sournoise offensive de la "paix blanché" va t'assaillir à ton tour,
Comme moi, tu dois tenir et vaincre, sois fort et malin.
Méfie-toi de l'hypocrisie boche.

Union des Grandes Associations Françaises
contre la propagande ennemie.
DEVAMBEZ GR.—PARIS.   VISA N°13.037

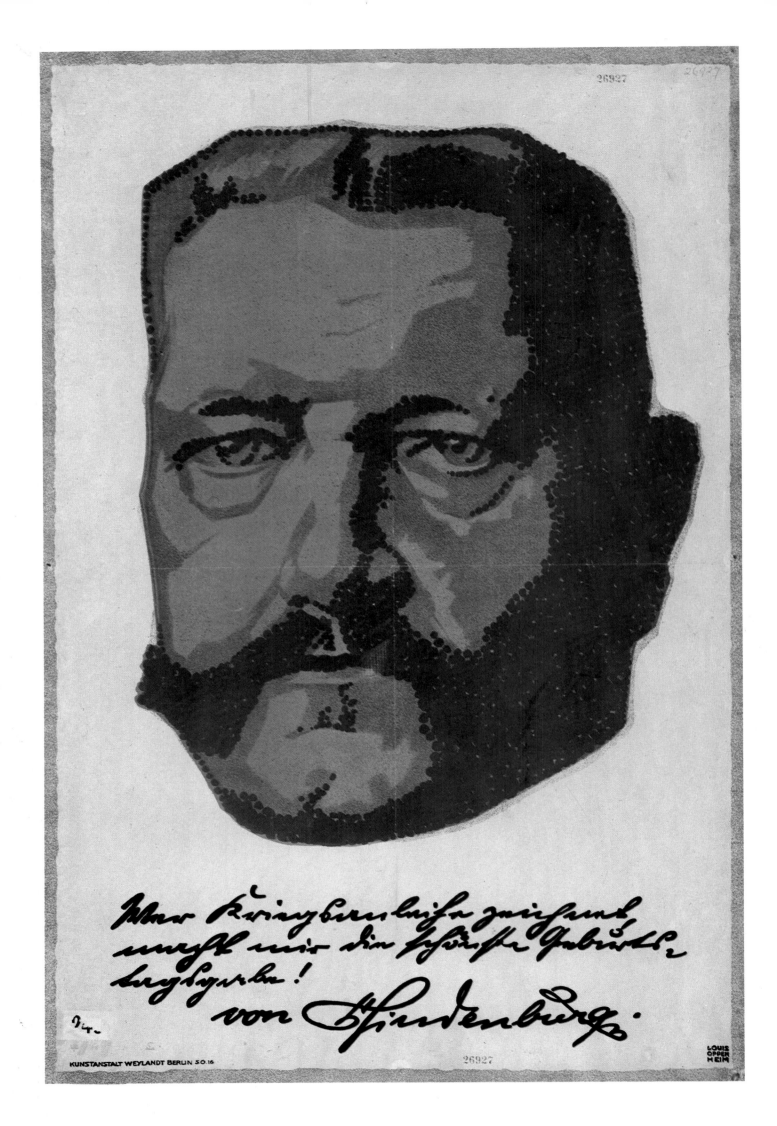

Louis Oppenheim: "von Hindenburg"

IOSEPH PENNELL DEL.

THAT LIBERTY SHALL NOT PERISH FROM THE EARTH BUY LIBERTY BONDS
FOURTH LIBERTY LOAN

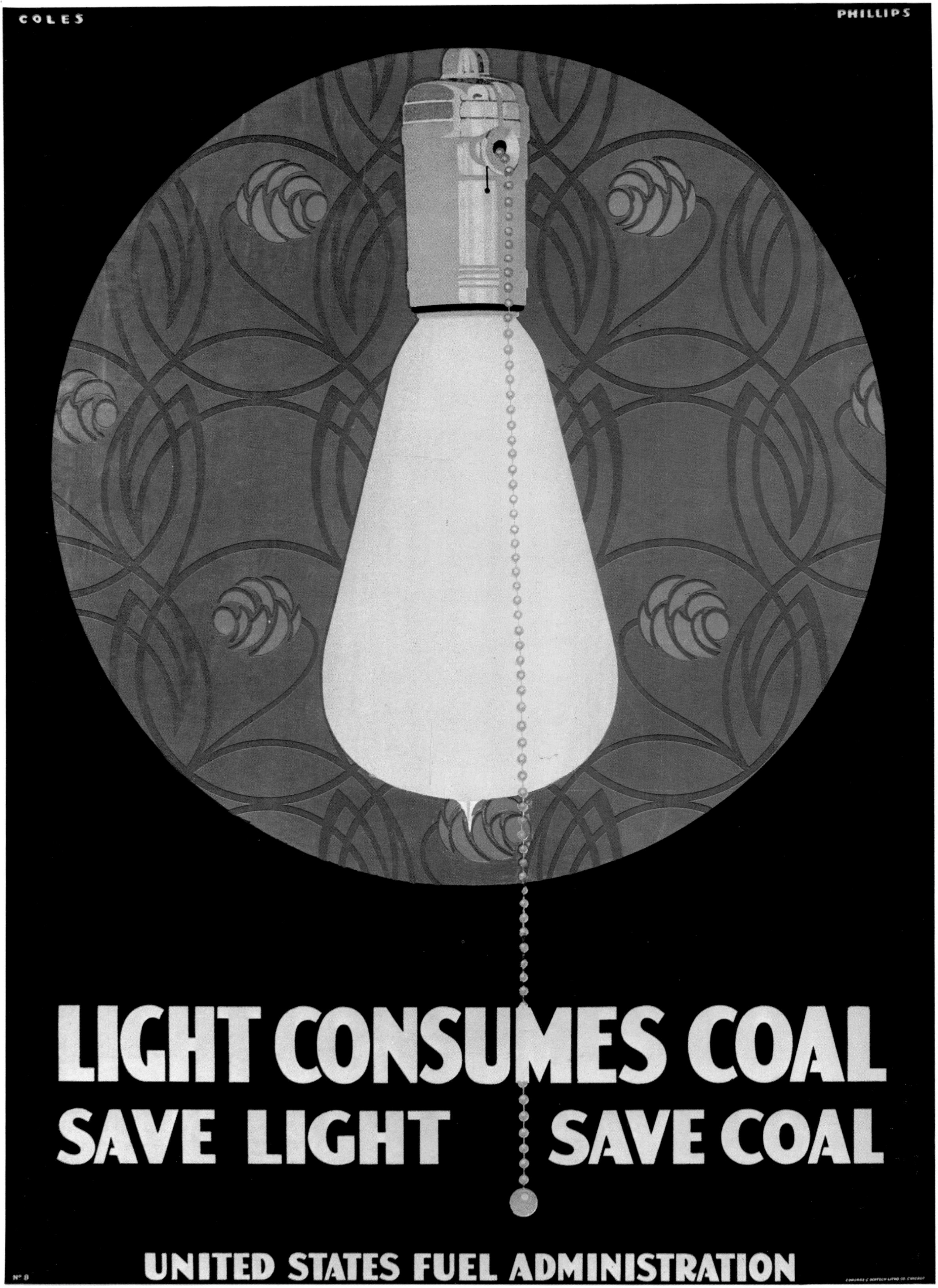
COLES
PHILLIPS
LIGHT CONSUMES COAL
SAVE LIGHT
SAVE COAL
UNITED STATES FUEL ADMINISTRATION

IN BELGIUM

HELP

THE NATIONAL COMMITTEE FOR RELIEF IN BELGIUM.
TRAFALGAR BUILDINGS. TRAFALGAR SQUARE. LONDON.

ENLIST

Fred Spear

SAVE
SERBIA
OUR ALLY

SEND CONTRIBUTIONS TO
SERBIAN RELIEF COMMITTEE OF AMERICA,
70 FIFTH AVENUE, NEW YORK

LANDES-

KRIEGSFÜRSORGE-AUSSTELLUNG

POZSONY JULI-AUGUST 1917

ANGERMAYER KÁROLY MÜINTÉZETE, POZSONY

169

ADOLPHE WILLETTE: "Charente Inférieure Week"   47

GIVE OR WE PERISH

AMERICAN COMMITTEE
FOR RELIEF IN THE NEAR EAST
ARMENIA ~ GREECE ~ SYRIA ~ PERSIA
CAMPAIGN *for* $30.000.000

Vier Wochen
neunte Kriegsanleihe –
vier Schicksalswochen
des Vaterlands!

=Deutscher!
Erkenne das Gebot
der Stunde:

Zeichne die Neunte
=Deutschland zur Wehr –
dem Feind zur Lehr'!

BERN
HARD

Graph. Kunstanstalt C.T. Wiskott, Breslau u. Berlin

THE ZEPPELIN RAIDS : THE VOW OF VENGEANCE
Drawn for 'The Daily Chronicle' by Frank Brangwyn A.R.A.

'DAILY CHRONICLE' READERS ARE COVERED AGAINST THE RISKS OF BOMBARDMENT BY ZEPPELIN OR AEROPLANE

The Underground Railways of London, knowing how many of their passengers are now engaged on important business in France and other parts of the world, send out this reminder of home. Thanks are due to George Clausen R.A. for the drawing.

A WISH   Mine be a cot beside the hill;
A bee-hive's hum shall soothe my ear;
A willowy brook that turns a mill,
With many a fall shall linger near.

The swallow, oft beneath my thatch
Shall twitter from her clay-built nest;
Oft shall the pilgrim lift the latch,
And share my meal, a welcome guest.

Around my ivied porch shall spring
Each fragrant flower that drinks the dew;
And Lucy, at her wheel, shall sing
In russet gown and apron blue.

The village church among the trees,
Where first our marriage vows were given,
With merry peals shall swell the breeze
And point with taper spire to Heaven.

Red Cross
Christmas
Roll Call
Dec. 16-23rd

The
GREATEST MOTHER
in the WORLD

Belgian Canal Boat Fund
For Relief of the Civil Population behind the firing Lines.
Send them Something.

Hassally.

The Sec, 71 Duke Street
Grosvenor Square, W.

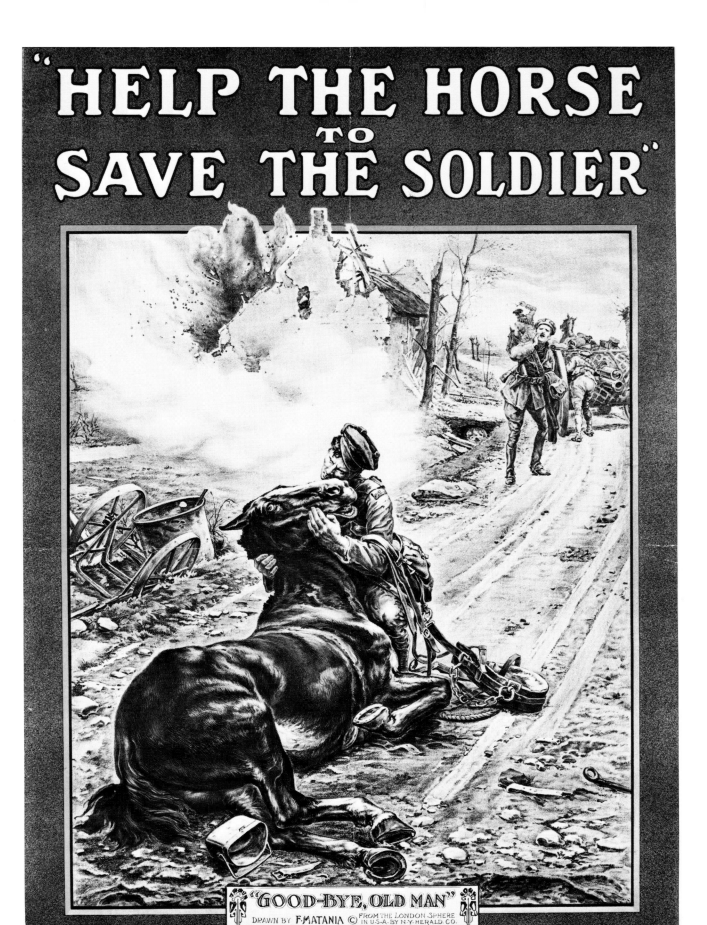

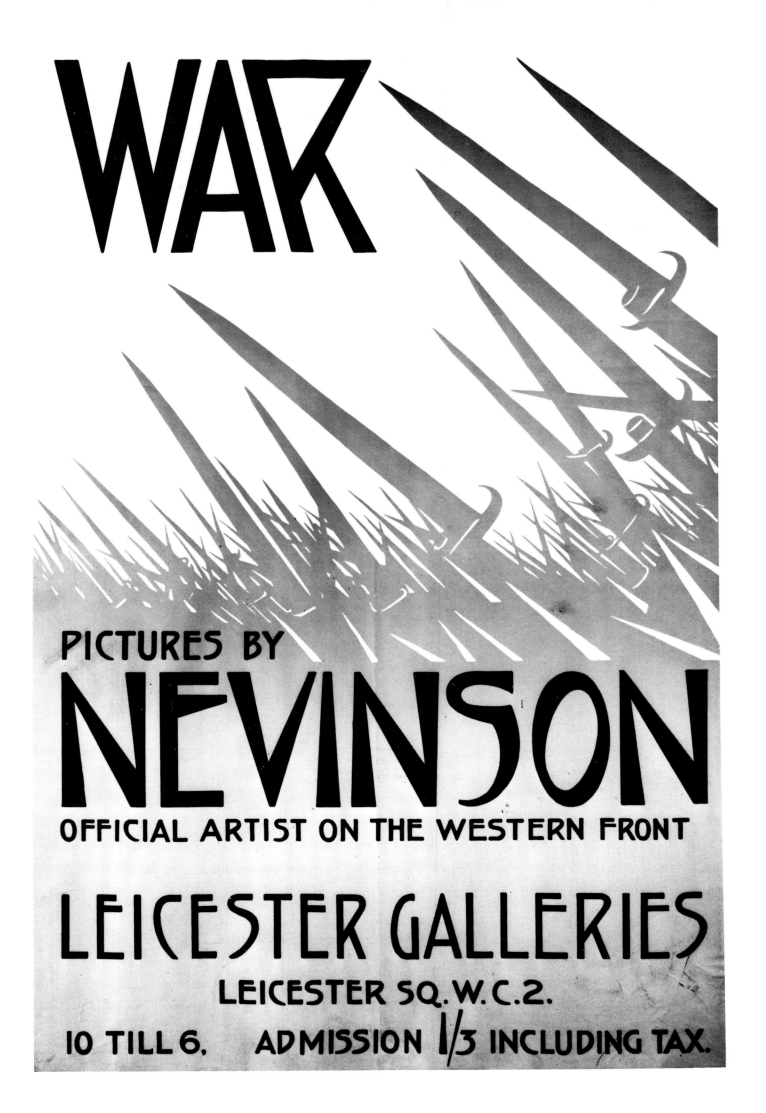

SOLDIERS ALL.

"TOMMY" *(home from the Front, to disaffected Workman).*
"WHAT'LD YOU THINK O' ME, MATE, IF I STRUCK
FOR EXTRA PAY IN THE MIDDLE OF AN ACTION?
WELL, THAT'S WHAT *YOU*'VE BEEN DOING."

Through Darkness
to Light

THE ONLY ROAD
FOR AN ENGLISHMAN

Through Fighting
to Triumph

JOHNSON, RIDDLE & CO., LTD., LONDON, S.E.

64 EMIL RANZENHOFER: "Subscribe to the Eighth War Loan"

UNION-BANK
8. KRIEGSANLEIHE

DURCH SIEG
ZUM FRIEDEN

70   THEODOR ZASCHE: "Union Bank"

72　Anonymous (Canadian)

71　Anonymous (British)

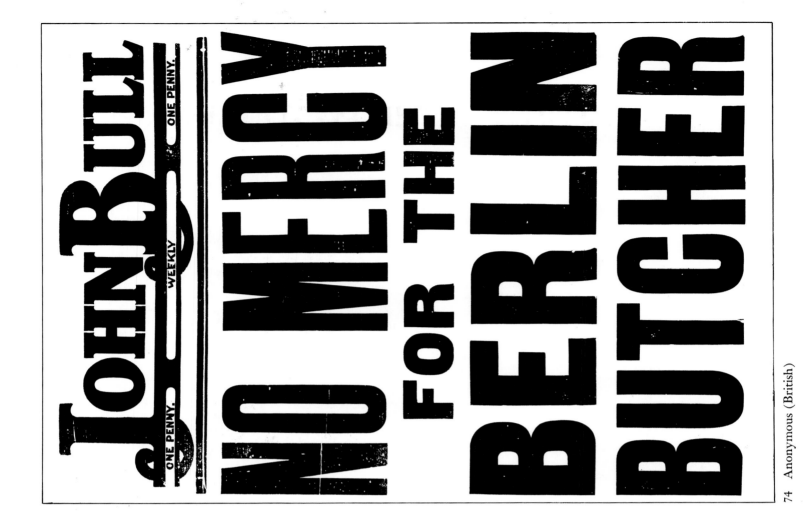

JOHN BULL

ONE PENNY. — WEEKLY — ONE PENNY.

NO MERCY
FOR THE
BERLIN
BUTCHER

74 Anonymous (British)

THE
SCRAP OF PAPER

Prussia's Perfidy—Britain's Bond.

The Treaty of 1839 (which the German Chancellor tore up, remarking that it was only "a scrap of paper") said:

"BELGIUM.... SHALL FORM AN INDEPENDENT AND PERPETUALLY NEUTRAL STATE. IT SHALL BE BOUND TO OBSERVE SUCH NEUTRALITY TOWARDS ALL OTHER STATES."

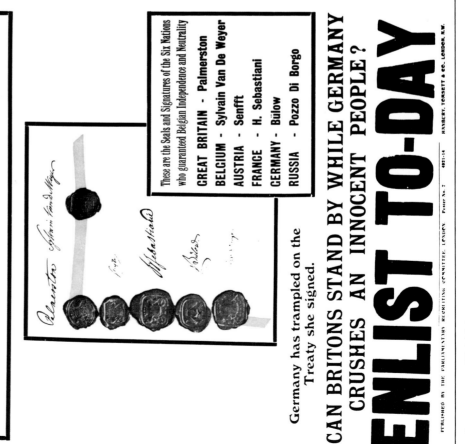

These are the Seals and Signatures of the Six Nations who guaranteed Belgian Independence and Neutrality

GREAT BRITAIN - Palmerston
BELGIUM - Sylvain Van De Weyer
AUSTRIA - Senfft
FRANCE - H. Sebastiani
GERMANY - Bülow
RUSSIA - Pozzo Di Borgo

Germany has trampled on the Treaty she signed.

CAN BRITONS STAND BY WHILE GERMANY CRUSHES AN INNOCENT PEOPLE?
ENLIST TO-DAY

PUBLISHED BY THE PARLIAMENTARY RECRUITING COMMITTEE, LONDON   Poster No. 7   4931-14   HANBURY, TOMSETT & CO. LONDON, N.W.

73 Anonymous (British)

THE ARTISTS & THE POSTERS

Frontispiece: SAVILE LUMLEY is best known for this poster which was designed for the printers Johnson, Riddle & Co. Its origin was recently explained by Mr. Paul Gunn in a letter to the Imperial War Museum:

> One night my father, so the story goes, came home very worried about the war situation and discussed with my mother whether he should volunteer. He happened to come in to where I was asleep and quite casually said to my mother, "If I don't join the forces whatever will I say to Paul if he turns round to me and says, 'What did you do in the Great War, Daddy?'" He suddenly turned round to my mother and said that would make a marvellous slogan for a recruiting poster. He shot off to see one of his pet artists, Savile Lumley, had a sketch drawn straight away, based on this theme projected about five years hence, although by the time it had taken shape the questioner had become one of my sisters. To end the story on a nice note, he joined the Westminster Volunteers a few days later!

1 MIHÁLY BIRÓ was born in Budapest on 30 November 1886, and studied in Budapest, Berlin, Paris and London. He became well known for posters of social protest, a famous one being that for the paper *Népszava* (People's Words), showing a worker swinging a hammer. Biró was active in the Hungarian revolutionary movement and became poster commissar of the shortlived Hungarian Socialist Republic in 1919. Subsequently he lived in Vienna, Berlin and America. He returned to Hungary in 1947, a very sick man, and died in Budapest on 30 November 1948.

This poster, dated 1917, advertises the newspaper *Pesti Napló* (Budapest Journal).

2 MARIO BORGONI was born at Pesaro on 24 July 1869. He studied in Naples and then specialized in poster design. This poster shows a characteristic figure in the Italian poster campaigns, in which appeals to workers were common.

Translation: "'At Last!' Sixth National Loan."

3 FRANK BRANGWYN was born in Bruges, Belgium, on 13 May 1867, the son of an architect. He studied art in London and worked for three years under William Morris before traveling in Europe and the East. Brangwyn was an outstanding mural painter, but also a prolific graphic artist and fine craftsman. His work is in many museums, including Brangwyn museums at Bruges and Orange (France), at Swansea (Wales) and the William Morris Gallery at Walthamstow. Brangwyn was knighted in 1941 and died in 1956. Among the best accounts of his art and character is *Brangwyn Pilgrimage* by his friend Albert de Belleroche (London, 1948). (No. 53 is also by Brangwyn.)

Brangwyn drew recruiting, charity and war loan posters in Britain, America and France. "Put Strength in the Final Blow" demonstrates his masterly lithographic technique. It was printed by the Avenue Press in London, where high standards were ensured by the supervision of F. E. Jackson.

4 T. BUTSCHKIN's well-known image is one of a group of Russian posters, produced before and after the Revolution, in the Imperial War Museum. Its aim was to provide funds for the new government, whose posters had a new democratic approach. It was probably printed in August 1917.

Translation: "Freedom Loan. [On with the] War Until Victory."

5 & 6 HOWARD CHANDLER CHRISTY was born in 1873 in Morgan County, Ohio. He studied in New York at the National Academy of Design and under the noted painter William Merritt Chase at the Art Students League. He became famous for the Christy Girls, the first of which appeared as an illustration called "The Soldier's Dream" in *Scribner's Magazine* at the time of the Spanish American War (the artist accompanied the United States troops to Cuba). After the First World War Christy gave more time to teaching and painting. His portrait sitters included Mrs. Calvin Coolidge, Mrs. William Randolph Hearst and Secretary of State Hughes. His most celebrated mural is *The Signing of the Constitution* in the Rotunda of the Capitol in Washington. He died in 1952.

Christy was one of several American illustrators whose prewar figures were used in First World War recruiting campaigns. "Gee!! I Wish I Were a Man" was produced in 1917, and was used on the back cover of *The Poster* in July of that year. The Red Cross poster, "The Spirit of America," typifies appeals made through images of women used in every country. A heroic, dignified figure is found equally in Europe and America, personifying country, liberty or freedom.

7 G. D. has not been further identified. This film poster, dated 1918, was bought for the Imperial War Museum in the following year.

Translation: "The Swiss Army."

8 HANS RUDI ERDT was born in Benediktbeuern, Bavaria, on 31 March 1883. He studied at the Munich School of Arts and Crafts, and became one of Berlin's foremost designers, working particularly for the printers Hollerbaum & Schmidt. Erdt died in 1918.

"U-Boote Heraus!" (U-Boats Out!) may advertise a film or a book about underwater warfare, increasingly important to Germany after the Battle of Jutland in 1916, when it had become apparent that the British blockade could not otherwise be broken. The strong single motif is typical of German poster design; the U particularly appealed to Erdt, who also used it in a poster for a wartime film about the Ukraine.

9 FRITZ ERLER was born at Frankenstein in Silesia (now Ząbkowice, Poland) on 15 December 1868. He studied at Breslau (now Wrocław) and in Paris before traveling in Italy and northern Germany. He was a co-founder of the magazine *Die Jugend*. Erler was a painter and his murals decorate many public buildings; the themes are often German folktales. He died in Munich on 11 July 1940.

Erler was haunted by the war. He wrote in 1917: "You pale apparitions, whitish like new fresco paintings, in the chalk hollows and corridors . . . you are always with me, you follow me until your real face becomes plain and you finally take shape as the man with the steel helmet before Verdun." This description might almost have been written for this poster, which was for the Sixth War Loan.

Translation: "Help Us Win! Subscribe to the War Loan."

10 WALTER H. EVERETT, whose work appeared in *The Saturday Evening Post* and *Scribner's Magazine*, was the designer of this poster, which made a special appeal to women. It was printed for the Fourth Liberty Loan in a million copies.

11 JULES ABEL FAIVRE was born in Lyons on 30 March 1867. He studied in Lyons and in Paris. After traveling in Turkey and Palestine he returned to become a well-known cartoonist, working for magazines like *Le Rire* and *Echo de Paris*. He was also a respected painter and portraitist. Faivre contributed posters to all the campaigns for French war loans. He died in Paris in August 1945.

"On les aura!" was a phrase coined by General Pétain during the Battle of Verdun. The poster was originally issued for the Second War Loan, but the design was reused and also plagiarized in Italy. The pose of the soldier recalls the famous sculptured group by François Rude on the Arc de Triomphe, which the sculptor later varied in a work commemorating Marshal Ney. Faivre's original drawing is in the Musée de la Guerre, Paris.

Translation: "We Will Get Them! Second National Defense Loan. Subscribe."

12 CHARLES BUCKLES FALLS was born in Fort Wayne, Indiana, on 10 December 1874. Falls was a prolific illustrator whose work included advertising, cover illustrations and some murals, such as a series of historical portraits for the New York State Office at Albany. He is well known for an ABC book of colored woodcuts which has remained in print since the first publication in 1923. Falls died on 15 April 1960.

"Books Wanted" succeeded in its object, and gained a considerable reputation for Falls, who had prepared the design in twenty-four hours. It was issued by the American Library Association.

13 JAMES MONTGOMERY FLAGG was born at Pelham Manor, Westchester County, New York, on 18 June 1877. He was a prodigy. He contributed to *St. Nicholas Magazine* when he was twelve, and two years later was drawing for *Judge* and *Life*. Flagg studied in New York, England and Paris. On his return be became a well-known and successful illustrator. Flagg wrote and illustrated several books, including *Celebrities* (1951), caricatures and portraits with comments by the artist. He died in 1960.

"I Want You for U.S. Army" is the best-known American poster of all time. It has been estimated that more than five million copies and reproductions have been printed. As time goes by, the image takes on new symbolic and metaphorical meanings. Flagg drew himself as Uncle Sam, but the pose is taken from the Kitchener poster by Alfred Leete (No. 25). Flagg did 46 war posters and also wrote and directed a film for the Red Cross.

14 DOMINIQUE CHARLES FOUQUERAY was born at Le Mans on 23 April in a year given variously as 1869, 1871 and 1872. He studied at the Ecole des Beaux-Arts in Paris. Fouqueray was a distinguished mural painter and a prolific illustrator for magazines like *L'Illustration*. His paintings are in important French museums, and several of his murals are in public buildings. He died in 1956.

Cardinal Mercier was a spokesman for the Belgian people in opposing the deportation of Belgian workmen and in condemning the German burning of the Louvain library. This poster was drawn in 1916, and helped to contribute to the Cardinal's reputation. Fouqueray was responsible for a number of war posters which show a mastery of lithographic technique.

Translation: "Cardinal Mercier Protects Belgium."

15 MALCOLM GIBSON was a Canadian designer whose poster of "Canadian Wheat" is a fair example of that country's wartime graphic production.

Translation: "Canadian Wheat. To Sell Our Wheat, We Must Subscribe to the Victory Loan."

16 JULIUS GIPKENS was born in Hanover on 16 February 1883. Gipkens had a wide-ranging design practice in Berlin. As a designer he was self-taught, although he learned much from the example of Lucian Bernhard (Nos. 50 & 51).

This poster for an exhibition of captured aircraft is one of Gipkens' finest designs. It was produced in two sizes for this exhibition and later used for another exhibition in 1918. Gipkens' war work was extensive, and included a number of interesting posters on the theme of conserving resources. (No. 57 is also by Gipkens.)

Translation: "German Captured Aircraft Exhibition. Patron: H.R.H. Prince Henry of Prussia. March 1917 at the [Berlin] Zoo." The word *Delka* is an abbreviation formed from *DEutsche LuftKriegsbeute Ausstellung*.

17 FRANZ GRIESSLER practiced as a poster designer in Austria, until he moved to South America. One of his posters, with a similarly simplified design, is included in an anthology of outstanding Austrian posters published in 1957.

Translation: "Navy Show 1918, in the Main Avenue of the Prater [chief park] in Vienna, 2 Minutes from the Praterstern. Completely New Program. Performances Begin at 5."

18 HANSI, whose real name was Jean Jacques Waltz, was born on 23 February 1873 at Colmar in Alsace. Hansi studied at Lyons, and returned to write and illustrate articles and books ridiculing the German authorities in his native Alsace and Lorraine. His satirical work led to his condemnation for high treason at Leipzig in 1914, but he jumped bail and fled to Switzerland. At the beginning of the war he joined the French army, and was transferred to propaganda work, of which he gave an account in *A Travers les Lignes Ennemies*, written with E. Tonnelat (1922). Hansi succeeded his father as curator of the Colmar museum in 1923. His successful career was interrupted by the war; in April 1941 he was attacked in the street and left for dead by two men believed to be from the Gestapo. Again he fled, returning to Colmar in 1945. He died there in 1951.

This poster is typical of Hansi's popular style, based on the brightly colored catchpenny prints widespread in nineteenth-century France, and generally called *images d'Epinal* after the town in Lorraine especially noted for producing them. Hansi was one of several French artists who used this style for propaganda during the war. He was particularly successful in portraying Alsace as a fairytale land under French rule. The poster included here, which contains a vision of the Strasbourg cathedral flying the French flag, appeared after the armistice.

Translation: " 'This heaven is our blue sky, this field is our land! This Lorraine and this Alsace are ours!' . . . Victor Hugo."

19 JOHN HASSALL was born in Walmer, near Deal in Kent, in 1868, the son of a naval officer. He studied painting in Antwerp and Paris, after which he made a living for a time as a black-and-white artist. He then turned to poster design; he had a contract for seven years with the printers David Allen, through which he achieved a considerable reputation, both for theatrical and commercial posters. Hassall also illustrated many children's books. He died in 1948. (No. 58 is also by Hassall.)

"Follow the Drum" is in his characteristic blend of bold outlines and bright colors. It might almost be a poster for a Christmas show.

20 & 21 LUDWIG HOHLWEIN was born at Wiesbaden on 26 April 1874. He began his career as a poster designer in 1906, after study as an architect. His commercial practice in Munich partly reflects the work of the Beggarstaffs (the British artists

Nicholson and Pryde), whose flat-pattern technique he much admired. His highly successful postwar practice included political work, and he designed posters for the Nazis during the 1939–1945 war. Hohlwein died in 1949.

The "Volksspende" poster is one of Hohlwein's best-known designs. Translation: "People's Charity for German Prisoners of War and Civil Internees." His "Dallkolat" poster shows how commercial products in every country were publicized by using references to the war. In some cases even the name of a product was designed or altered to appeal to patriots. Translation: "Endurance, Strength and Energy. Kola-Dallmann Dallkolat [a candy]. Tried and Proven in the Army for 25 Years."

22 LUCIEN-HECTOR JONAS was born at Anzin (Département du Nord) on 8 April 1880. He studied at Valenciennes and Paris. Jonas became a successful illustrator, contributing to *Le Journal*. His illustrative work includes cartoons, well-known images of the war and book illustrations. His work is also represented in public collections and public buildings. Jonas died in Paris in 1947.

Translation: "African Army and Colonial Forces Day."

23 ADOLF KARPELLUS was born at Neu-Sandec in Galicia (now Nowy Sącz, Poland) in 1869, the son of an Austrian major. Karpellus studied at Vienna and in Paris. He was a painter and a poster designer. He died in Vienna in 1919.

Karpellus produced a number of war posters, some of whose designs were also used for postcards. This seventh war loan poster is one of Karpellus' best, typical of the decorative style of Austrian art at this time. The dove, symbolizing the peace obtainable through the victory made possible by war loans, was a frequent motif.

Translation: "Subscribe to the Seventh War Loan."

24 JULIUS KLINGER, who has been called "the moving spirit of the Vienna poster designers," was born in Vienna in 1876. He studied there, and then worked as an illustrator, turning to poster design in 1897. During the First World War his practice was in Berlin. His work for the printing firm Hollerbaum & Schmidt was extremely successful. By that time Klinger had turned away from the Art Nouveau style, refining his designs to flat decorative forms in clear colors and accompanied by a precise lettering. He aimed to make the poster a symbol. Klinger received several important commissions from the Austrian Republic after the war. He also designed typefaces and published a number of books.

The poster included here was presumably based on Willy Menz's Sixth German War Loan poster of the previous year.

Translation: "Eighth War Loan."

25 ALFRED LEETE was born in Thorpe Achurch, Northampton, on 28 August 1882, the son of a farmer. He was a humorous illustrator who also designed posters, for example for the London Underground. He died in London in 1933.

The famous Kitchener design first appeared on the cover of the weekly magazine *London Opinion* for 5 September 1914. In this original form it bore the slogan "Your Country Needs You." It was the most famous and successful poster produced by the Parliamentary Recruiting Committee. There were many different versions, and it inspired many imitations, of which the most famous is Flagg's "I Want You for U.S. Army" (No. 13). Leete's original drawing is in the Imperial War Museum.

26 HEINRICH LEFLER was born in Vienna in 1863, the son of an artist. Lefler studied in Vienna and Munich. He was a decorative painter who was a leading member of the Secession group (Viennese Art Nouveau), but left it to found the Hagenbund with Josef Urban.

The two-headed eagle, which is one of Austria's national symbols, was a characteristically decorative motif for Lefler to use. The frieze in this poster reflects both Lefler's practice as an interior designer, and the geometric heraldic style current in Vienna.

Translation: "Subscribe to the Fourth War Loan."

27 OTTO LEHMANN's poster is one of the few German posters to be included and praised in Hardie and Sabin's work about posters of the First World War (*War Posters*, London, 1920). It is a particularly successful use of a symbol destroyed. Lehmann was born in 1865.

Translation: "Support Our Men in Uniform [literally, Men in Field Gray]. Rend England's Might. Subscribe to the War Loan." Note the typographical error in the word *zerreisst*.

28 MAXIMILIAN LENZ was born in Vienna in 1860. He studied in Vienna and held a Rome scholarship for two years. He was a painter and lithographer, a member of the Viennese Secession. Lenz died in 1948.

Lenz designed several war posters during the 1914–1918 war. The image of St. George and the Dragon was also used by other countries as a convenient symbol for good and evil. There is a British recruiting poster (No. 71) with this theme which was issued before 1916, whereas this poster was issued in 1917. Plagiarism was common practice for poster designers, but the variation of design makes Lenz's version far superior.

Translation: "Subscribe to the Sixth War Loan."

29 & 30 JOSEPH CHRISTIAN LEYENDECKER was born at Montabaur (near Koblenz) in Germany on 23 March 1874. He lived in the United States from 1883. Leyendecker studied in Chicago and Paris, whence he returned to practice as an illustrator in the United States. Leyendecker was famous for his covers for *The Saturday Evening Post* between 1900 and 1940, and he was the originator of the Arrow Collar Man, the well-known publicity campaign. Leyendecker died on 25 July 1951.

The coal poster was one of many done for the Division of Pictorial Publicity, which supplied designs free to government departments. *The Poster* commented: "This virile poster, which aids the work of the United States Fuel Administration, is one of the best that have had their origin in the war. It is by J. C. Leyendecker, the original being done in oils. The lithograph . . . faithfully discloses every detail of the artist's work."

The poster for the Third Liberty Loan was specially requested as a recognition of the successful promotion of the war loans by the American Boy Scouts.

31 NORMAN ALFRED WILLIAM LINDSAY was born in Creswick, Victoria, Australia, on 23 February 1879. At sixteen he drew sporting illustrations for a Melbourne paper, and in 1901 joined the *Sydney Bulletin*, where he became chief cartoonist. Lindsay was a prolific book illustrator and well known as a painter. He published an autobiographical book, *My Mask*, in 1957, and a biography has appeared recently. Lindsay died on 21 November 1969.

"?" was one of six posters that Lindsay designed for the last Australian recruiting campaign. On a prearranged night, "?", which had been widely and secretly distributed, was pasted up throughout Australia. The second poster of the campaign followed, and then others at intervals of seven to ten days. But before the last two posters were issued the armistice was signed, and the campaign abandoned. The savage tone of the posters was deliberate; Lindsay held that "A country that kills the killer in man would be destroyed by any other country which has preserved the instinct to kill."

32 LUCIANO ACHILLE MAUZAN, born in 1883, is best known for an adaptation of Alfred Leete's Kitchener poster which shows an Italian soldier pointing at the spectator. It was an appeal for funds for a war loan, which was widely used. It is to be seen among the photographs in Rubetti's books on Italian war-loan campaigns showing the posters displayed in

different Italian towns. Mauzan practiced in Milan after the war.

The poster included here shows a giant enemy hand stretching toward the River Piave. Mauzan's work is in the mainstream of Italian commercial art, but in this case he has drawn inspiration from the fantasies in book illustrations. Such strange images are relatively rare in war posters. The poster was issued by the Consorzio Bancario (Banking Consortium).

Translation: "For Liberation, Subscribe!"

33 MAURICE NEUMONT was born in Paris on 22 September 1868. He studied under the celebrated academician Gérôme. Neumont became a noted illustrator; during the war he organized a canteen in Paris for artists and the families of artists serving in the forces, before working on camouflage and for propaganda. Neumont died on 10 February 1930.

The poster's symbol of a *poilu* who shouts "They shall not pass!" was commisioned by the Union des Grandes Associations Françaises against German interests. The treatment of this theme is worth comparing with David Wilson's "Once a German" (No. 69).

Translation: "They shall not pass! 1914–1918. Twice I have stood fast and conquered on the Marne, my brother civilian. A deceptive 'peace offensive' will attack you in your turn; like me, you must stand firm and conquer. Be strong and shrewd. Beware of Boche hypocrisy."

34 LOUIS OPPENHEIM was born at Coburg on 4 May 1879. He studied in London, where he worked as a caricaturist and advertising artist for several years, until his return to Germany in 1906. His work is much influenced by the Beggarstaffs. From 1908 he became a well-known designer in Berlin. Oppenheim gave further support to Hindenburg in the 1932 election campaign.

Oppenheim worked extensively for the war effort in Germany, doing many diagrammatic posters as well as more dramatic designs, such as this Hindenburg poster for the Seventh War Loan. Hindenburg's head was used as a poster motif by several designers, but Oppenheim's image is especially powerful.

Text: "Wer Kriegsanleihe zeichnet, macht mir die schönste Geburtstagsgabe! . . . von Hindenburg." Translation: "The man who subscribes to the War Loan is giving me the finest birthday present! . . . von Hindenburg."

35 JOSEPH PENNELL was born in Philadelphia in 1857, where he studied. Pennell was a fine black-and-white artist, well known for his architectural drawings. He wrote extensively about the graphic arts, and published an autobiography. During the war Pennell drew a series of lithographs of industrial work, and became associated with the production of posters for the Division of Pictorial Publicity after 1917. Pennell died in Brooklyn, New York, on 23 April 1926.

"That Liberty Shall Not Perish from the Earth" was a poster for the Fourth Liberty Loan. A short account of the production of the poster was published by Pennell in 1918 which describes the different printing methods used, including a rather unsuccessful gravure for a magazine of which the Imperial War Museum also has a copy. The title of the poster was not Pennell's; he had wanted "Buy Liberty Bonds or You Will See This." Half a million copies of the poster were distributed.

36 CLARENCE COLES PHILLIPS was born in Springfield, Ohio, in 1880, and moved to New York in 1905. After working for a radiator company, he began to run an advertising agency and turned to advertising and illustration himself. The hallmark of his magazine covers was, the Fadeaway Girl; in these covers a good-looking girl's dress was made to merge into the flat background of the picture. Phillips died in 1929.

The poster here illustrated is a typically well-thought out design, the strong pattern of which recalls Art Nouveau.

37 FRANCISQUE POULBOT was born at St.-Denis, near Paris, in 1879. Poulbot was a humorous artist who specialized in cartoons of charming and irreverent children, especially in the Montmartre neighborhood. He published two books of cartoons before the First World War, and was a constant book illustrator. He died in Paris in 1946.

The theatrical production advertised in the poster included here was written with Paul Gsell. The drawing is typical of Poulbot's style. He used this motif of children in other war posters, mainly for charity days, but also for the war loan of 1916.

Translation: "Under the patronage of the French Secretariat of Liberated Villages. Arts Theater. *The Kids in the Ruins* by Paul Gsell and Poulbot. Popular song by Déodat de Sévérac. Sets by Poulbot, Lefol and Carré."

38 VOJTECH PRESSIG was born in 1873 in what is now Czechoslovakia. He studied in Prague and Paris. Eventually he headed the Department of Printing and Graphic Arts at the Wentworth Institute, Boston (see the initials "WI, P&GA" on the poster). In 1931 he returned to Czechoslovakia.

The poster shown here, much closer in design to a European style than to American illustration, was one of a set produced for the Czecho-Slovak Recruiting Office in New York. Pressig directed his Wentworth Institute students in the designing of the poster.

39 LOUIS RAEMAEKERS was born at Roermond in Holland on 6 April 1869. He studied in Amsterdam, Brussels and Paris. At first a painter, he turned cartoonist in 1909, working for *De Telegraaf*. Raemaekers was an outstanding propagandist during the war, his cartoons and posters enjoying a wide distribution. He died at Scheveningen, near The Hague, on 26 July 1956.

Raemaekers' anti-German cartoons became so widely known that in 1916 he moved to England to work more easily for the Allied Press. "In Belgium—Help" was probably produced soon after this date for the National Committee for Relief in Belgium, whose first annual report stated that they had distributed 185,000 posters. The design was also used for two of the Committee's leaflet covers.

40 J. ALLEN ST. JOHN was born in Chicago on 1 October 1872. He studied in New York and Paris.

This anti-German poster typifies the hate campaign which arose in America after the country's entry into the war. The motif of a bloody handprint is also found in French posters.

41 LINA VON SCHAUROTH was born in Frankfurt on 9 December 1875. She studied under Trübner and Hohlwein and practiced as a painter, graphic artist and stained-glass designer. Her eighty-fifth birthday was celebrated by an exhibition at Limpurg House in Frankfurt.

The poster shown here is typical of Schauroth's sombre, rich colors and her bold designs of rounded forms.

Translation: "Emperor's and People's Thank Offering for the Army and Navy. Frankfurt Christmas Gift, 1917. Donations Accepted at Bureau 5, Theaterplatz 14."

42 GEORGE-BERTIN SCOTT DE PLAGNOLLES was born in Paris on 10 June 1873. Scott was a pupil of Edouard Detaille, and became a successful painter and official portraitist, whose sitters included several sovereigns and Mussolini. He drew for *L'Illustration* and painted a number of pictures of the war, following the Balkan campaign as reporter-illustrator.

Translation: "For the Flag! For Victory! Subscribe to the National Loan. Subscriptions Are Accepted in Paris and the Provinces at the National Credit Bank."

43 FRED SPEAR produced this poster for the Boston Committee of Public Safety after the *Lusitania* had been sunk by a German U-boat in 1915. More than 1,000 civilian lives were lost, 128 of them American. The poster recalls the loss of an American mother and child.

The *Lusitania* sinking was widely used by both sides in the war for propaganda. This included a German medallion, of which the British produced a counterfeit, interpreting the sinking as a premeditated attack on civilians. The German interpretation was that the ship had carried munitions. The destruction of the *Lusitania* was a factor in America's decision to enter the war.

Many Americans joined the forces of the belligerent nations before America's entry into the war in 1917. It is estimated that more than 15,000 Americans enlisted in the Canadian forces, and the Lafayette squadron of the French Air Force was noted for its American aces.

44 THÉOPHILE-ALEXANDRE STEINLEN was born in Lausanne on 10 November 1859. He studied in Paris, where he began designing book covers, music covers and posters. Some of these realistic designs had success comparable to that of the decorative work of Jules Chéret or Willette. Steinlen was a prolific book illustrator who specialized in genre subjects and liked drawing cats. He died in Paris on 14 December 1923.

Steinlen's war posters were mainly for the relief of distress in different countries. The crowd scene in this "Save Serbia" poster, drawn for an American campaign, echoes some of the realist drawings of groups of workers in his book illustrations. (No. 67 is also by Steinlen).

45 PÁL SUJÁN was born in Budapest on 5 May 1880. He studied in Budapest and later became a drawing teacher in Pozsony (then in Hungary, now Bratislava in Czechoslovakia). His work was widely shown, mostly portraits and figure paintings.

The poster illustrated here is the only one by Suján in the Imperial War Museum. The Pointillist technique used in the landscape suggests familiarity with the work of that French school, whereas the outlines of the landscape recall the work of Van Gogh.

Translation: "National War Relief Exhibition, Pozsony, July-August 1917. Opening 18 July."

46 WALTER WHITEHEAD was born in Chicago on 2 September 1874. He studied under Howard Pyle, and taught at the Chicago Academy of Fine Arts.

The well-known poster "Come On!" was produced for the Fourth Liberty Loan.

47 ADOLPHE WILLETTE was born at Châlons-sur-Marne in 1857. He was a charming draughtsman who contributed to many periodicals, such as *Le Courrier Français, Le Chat Noir* and *Le Rire*, besides painting decorations for several cabarets. He is known for pictures of pierrots, harlequins and columbines, but also for effective satirical drawings. Willette died in Paris on 4 February 1926.

Translation: "1917. Charente-Inférieure Week. Long Live the Nation!" Charente-Inférieure was the old name of Charente-Maritime, the Atlantic Coast French *département* in which La Rochelle is located.

48 ALFRED AARON WOLMARK was born in Warsaw on 28 December 1877. His family went to England in 1883. Wolmark studied in London, where from 1911 he became a stage designer, notably for the Diaghilev ballet, and a painter with a slowly increasing reputation. He died on 6 January 1961.

The poster shown here exemplifies Wolmark's abstract pattern-making. The strong color contrasts are reminiscent of his painting, which owed much to the vivid simplifications of artists like Van Gogh and Gauguin. The Russian words on the poster mean: "Russian Exhibition."

49 WLADYSLAW THEODORE BENDA was born in 1873 in Posen (then in Prussia, now Poznań, Poland) and studies at Cracow Academy. In 1899 he emigrated to the United States, where he became well known as an illustrator and, after the 1914–1918 war, as a maker of masks. Benda masks were used in theatrical productions and photographed on *Vogue* models by Edward Steichen. Benda tells the story in *Masks*, published in 1944 in New York, where he died in 1948.

"Give or We Perish" is typical of the romantic approach of Benda's wartime posters, which included three recruiting posters for Polish patriots in America.

50 & 51 LUCIAN BERNHARD was born in Vienna on 15 March 1883. He studied in Munich and Berlin. His career as a poster designer began with a winning design for Priester matches in 1905. Bernhard's visual method was to associate a single image with the name of a product, much in the same way as Cappiello designed posters in Paris. Bernhard was a prominent poster designer in Berlin until 1923, when he settled in New York, where he died on 29 May 1972. His work included interior designing and furniture design.

Bernhard's many war posters were mainly for war loans. "Das ist der Weg zum Frieden" was for the Seventh War Loan. The typography is in the face called Fraktur, which Bernhard himself designed, and is matched by the mailed fist in a technique which recalls medieval woodcuts. Translation: "This is the way to peace—the enemy wills it so! Therefore subscribe to the war loan!"

"Vier Wochen" was for the Ninth War Loan. Translation: "Four weeks of the Ninth War Loan—four fateful weeks for our country! People of Germany! Recognize the commandment of the hour: Subscribe to the Ninth, for the defense of Germany—as a lesson to the enemy!"

52 FRITZ BOEHLE was born at Emmendingen (near Freiburg im Breisgau, Germany) on 7 February 1873. He studied in Frankfurt and Munich. In 1896 he moved to Frankfurt, where he practiced until his death on 20 October 1916.

Boehle's work is strongly influenced by German Renaissance art, and this poster owes a particular debt to Dürer, whose engraving "St. George" (1508) is similar in composition.

Translation: "Thanks be to God. Givest thou a mite, be it ne'er so small, thou shalt be blessed by God."

53 On FRANK BRANGWYN see No. 3.

"The Zeppelin Raids" was specially drawn for *The Daily Chronicle* and used as a poster on the London Underground. The image of a Zeppelin was powerfully emotive, and it is interesting that in Brangwyn's charity posters, such as the one he did for orphans, he used an equally dominant image in the background, only in that case a cross.

54 GEORGES LOUIS CAPON, born 1890, was a painter and decorative artist who was jointly responsible with Dorival for several war posters. GEORGES DORIVAL was born on 5 November 1879. He studied at the Ecole Nationale des Arts Décoratifs, and became editor of *L'Art et la Mode*. He designed posters especially for the railways and shipping lines.

The strong silhouette treatment of "2 Fléaux" is unusual in French war posters, which are more often fine lithographic drawings, like the work of Steinlen or Fouqueray. The American commission responsible for this poster would have recalled the successful health campaigns using posters in several American cities before and during the war.

Translation: "Two scourges: the Boche, tuberculosis. The Boche eagle will be defeated. Tuberculosis must also be defeated."

55 GEORGE CLAUSEN was born in London on 18 April 1852, the son of a decorative painter, whose firm he entered to become a furniture designer. In 1873 he won a scholarship to the South Kensington School of Art, where he studied until 1875, afterwards becoming assistant to the painter Edwin Long. Clausen is best known for pictures of rural scenes; he was a prominent Royal Academician, knighted in 1927, and painted one of the large commemorative pictures intended for the Imperial War Museum's Hall of Remembrance, never built. Clausen died on 23 November 1944.

"A Wish" was one of four posters sent by the Underground Railways of London to British troops overseas in 1916. They proved popular decorations, for example in messes and Y.M.C.A. huts. Clausen was one of four artists who provided free designs for these posters. The fine lettering may be the work of Clausen's daughter, who studied under Edward Johnston, designer of the famous London Underground typeface.

56 ALONZO EARL FORINGER was born on 1 February 1878 at Kaylor, Armstrong County, Pennsylvania. He studied in Pittsburgh and New York. He was a mural painter, illustrator and designer of banknotes. Foringer died on 9 December 1948.

"The Greatest Mother in the World" was an outstandingly successful poster, much reprinted. Its appeal lies in religious associations with the Virgin and Child. The poster was produced for the Division of Advertising, and was used both during the war, and in December 1918 for the Red Cross Christmas Roll Call, aiming to enroll every American with the slogan "All you need is a heart and a dollar!" The model for the nurse was an artist, Agnes Tait.

57 On JULIUS GIPKENS see No. 16.

Gipkens' poster appealing for beechnuts is an example of an interesting group of posters calling for the conservation of resources including food, metals and human hair. These posters have a humorous tone unlike the war loan campaigns, which are more purely patriotic. There is an interesting contrast between the First World War and the Second World War. Humor was a keynote of American and British posters from 1939 to 1945, though rare in the First World War.

Translation: "If You Want Oil, Gather Beechnuts. Wartime Committee on Oils and Fats."

58 On JOHN HASSALL see No. 19.

"Belgian Canal Boat Fund" is unusual in Hassall's work because of its delicate technique and pathos. It was one of the designs done free by the artist for charities during the war. The Belgian Canal Boat Fund gave food, clothing and medical aid to civilians behind the lines in Belgium and sent comforts to Belgian soldiers. The original intention to send these supplies by the canals was abandoned.

59 FORTUNINO MATANIA was born in Naples on 16 April 1881. He was trained in his father's studio. Before the war Matania established himself an an illustrator, working especially for *The Sphere*, for which magazine he traveled widely. His work became well known in Europe and America, and during the 1930s he also designed posters. He exhibited paintings, many of which are in regimental collections in Britain. He died in London in February 1963.

Matania's war illustrations are more often reconstructions of events than eye-witness accounts, although he was on the front in the 1914–1918 war. His drawing "Good-Bye, Old Man," which originally appeared in *The Sphere*, is a characteristic example of the sentiment of the period, executed with typically detailed draughtsmanship.

60 PAUL NASH was born on 11 May 1889 in Kensington (London). He studied in London and became known as a landscape artist. Nash's visionary landscapes and illustrations make him one of the most distinguished British painters of the century. Nash died on 11 July 1946 at Boscombe, Hampshire.

The torn landscape of this poster is characteristic of Nash's themes on the Western Front, which he took up in major paintings such as *The Menin Road*.

61 CHRISTOPHER RICHARD WYNNE NEVINSON was born in Hampstead (London) on 13 August 1889, son of a journalist. He studied architecture and then painting, being at the Slade art school from 1912 to 1913, before working in Paris. Nevinson was closely associated with the Futurists. He served in France from 1914 to 1916 with the Red Cross and the Royal Army Medical Corps, before being invalided out. He was appointed as an official war artist in 1917. Nevinson exhibited widely, and wrote an autobiographical book, *Paint and Prejudice* (1937). He died in London on 7 October 1946.

The poster included here was used to advertise an exhibition in March 1918. The design was copied for propaganda use and Nevinson wrote asking to whom he ought to *give* the design for the war bond campaign. "They seem to want it as I notice they are always cribbing it—and none too well—in some effect or another." The angular shapes and typography are Vorticist, and the composition, with bayonets against the sky, also occurs in Nevinson's paintings.

62 BERNARD PARTRIDGE was born in London on 11 October 1861. Partridge started as a stained-glass designer and painter, later turning to illustration, where he became known for his contributions to *Punch*. His main fame was as a political cartoonist. Partridge was knighted in 1925, and lived in London, where he died on 9 August 1945.

This *Punch* cartoon was a comment on the Clyde Engineers' strike of February 1915, settled in the following month. Cartoons and press illustrations were widely reproduced during the war, a practice followed in the Second World War.

63 GERALD SPENCER PRYSE was born in London in 1881. He studied in London and Paris, and became a watercolorist and lithographer. He exhibited widely and illustrated many books, living in later life in Morocco. He died on 28 November 1956.

"The Only Road for an Englishman" was published by the Underground Electric Railways, then under the direction of Frank Pick. Spencer Pryse drew directly on the lithographic stone for this work, as he had done for a series of lithographs, *The Autumn Campaign, 1914*, which he had executed when a dispatch rider for the Belgian government. Spencer Pryse's compassionate imagery was also used to good effect for a series of Labour Party election posters between 1910 and 1929.

64 EMIL RANZENHOFER was born in Vienna on 4 June 1864. He studied under Griepenkerl, and became a painter and engraver. This splendid calligraphic poster is an example of the best typographic design of the day. Ranzenhofer died in Berlin on 21 July 1916.

Translation: "Subscribe to the Eighth War Loan."

65 TONI SCHÖNECKER was born on 1 November 1893 in Falkenau bei Eger in Bohemia, then part of the Austro-Hungarian Empire, now in Czechoslovakia (Falkenau is now Sokolov, Eger is now Cheb). He studied in Vienna and Munich. He was responsible for several graffito decorative schemes, including the Leichenhalle (mortuary) in Falkenau, but mainly practiced as an illustrator and graphic artist. He died in 1945.

Translation: "Exhibition of the Aviators Aid Committee. Imperial Military Academy, Wiener Neustadt, 16–25 April 1916, 10–6 o'clock."

66 KARL SIGRIST was born in Stuttgart in 1885. He studied in Stuttgart and visited Italy before returning to practice as a designer when he was 24. This poster, with the dove of peace and the German eagle, was for the Eighth War Loan.

Translation: "Subscribe to the War Loan."

67 On THÉOPHILE-ALEXANDRE STEINLEN see No. 44.

"Sur la Terre Ennemie" is one of Steinlen's best-known and most pathetic posters. An appreciation in the *Gazette des Beaux Arts* particularly pointed out the sinister landscape of snow and darkness, the utter dejection of the prisoners and their staring eyes which seem unable to see any longer.

Translation: "On enemy soil Russian prisoners are dying of hunger."

68 I. VLADIMIROV was a painter of battle scenes and worked for newspapers before the war. This is the only poster by him owned by the Imperial War Museum; the Lenin Library in Moscow has a copy of this one and several others.

Translation: "Everyone must aid our glorious troops, and all who can must subscribe to the 5½% war loan."

69 DAVID WILSON was born at Minterburn Manse, Co. Tyrone (Northern Ireland), on 4 July 1873. He left employment in a Belfast bank for London, where he became well known as a newspaper cartoonist. Wilson, who also painted landscapes and watercolors, regularly exhibited at the Royal Academy. He died in 1935.

The poster illustrated was produced in January 1918 by the British Empire Union, founded to "destroy German influence, prohibit German labour and boycott German goods." It is typical of the anti-German posters produced in Britain during the war.

70 THEODOR ZASCHE was born in Vienna on 18 October 1862, the son of a miniature painter. He studied under his father, and became a newspaper cartoonist. He died in Vienna in 1922.

This elegant Art Nouveau design shows the style lingering throughout the war.

Translation: "Union Bank. Eighth War Loan. Through Victory to Peace."

71 St. George, the patron saint of England, was a natural choice for a poster motif. The designer of this poster is not known, but was possibly a draughtsman employed by the printing firm Eyre and Spottiswoode.

72 The Canadian mascot of a beaver is used in this poster for thrift stamps. WSS in the lower right-hand corner stands for War Savings Stamps.

73 The treaty guaranteeing Belgian neutrality was described by Bethmann-Hollweg as a "scrap of paper," to the intense indignation of the British. Many other notices and proclamations were used in propaganda, notably execution orders for spying and martial-law orders which were reprinted by the other side.

74 JOHN BULL was edited by Horatio Bottomley, responsible for a fierce anti-German campaign, both in this paper and from public platforms.